TRIANGLE HISTORIES
★★★★★ ★ ★★★★★

THE REVOLUTIONARY WAR

THE BATTLE OF
LONG ISLAND

Fountaindale Public Library District
300 West Briarcliff Road
Bolingbrook, IL 60440-2894
(630) 759-2102

Scott Ingram

BLACKBIRCH®
PRESS

THOMSON
———★———™
GALE

San Diego • Detroit • New York • San Francisco • Cleveland • New Haven, Conn. • Waterville, Maine • London • Munich

© 2004 by Blackbirch Press™. Blackbirch Press™ is an imprint of The Gale Group, Inc., a division of Thomson Learning, Inc.

Blackbirch Press™ and Thomson Learning™ are trademarks used herein under license.

For more information, contact
The Gale Group, Inc.
27500 Drake Rd.
Farmington Hills, MI 48331-3535
Or you can visit our Internet site at http://www.gale.com

ALL RIGHTS RESERVED
No part of this work covered by the copyright hereon may be reproduced or used in any form or by any means—graphic, electronic, or mechanical, including photocopying, recording, taping, Web distribution or information storage retrieval systems—without the written permission of the publisher.

Every effort has been made to trace the owners of copyrighted material.

Photo credits: cover, pages 11, 27 © CORBIS; page 5 © North Wind Picture Archives; pages 7, 10, 16, 24 © Bettman/CORBIS; pages 9, 15, 25, 28 © Hulton/Archive, Getty Images; page 12 © Bridgeman Art Library; page 14 © Francis G. Mayer/CORBIS; page 16 © New York Historical Society, New York, USA/Bridgeman Art Library; page 20 © Courtesy Delaware National Guard Heritage Committee; page 23 © Delaware Art Museum, Wilmington, USA/The Bridgeman Art Library; page 26 © Library of Congress

LIBRARY OF CONGRESS CATALOGING-IN-PUBLICATION DATA

Ingram, Scott (William Scott)
  The Battle of Long Island / by Scott Ingram.
    v. cm. — (Triangle history of the American Revolution series. Revolutionary War battles)
Includes bibliographical references (p.) and index.
Contents: "A most vigorous push" — Meeting at the middle colonies — Battle lines are drawn — The Battle of Long Island — The miraculous escape.
  ISBN 1-56711-776-7 (alk. paper)
  1. Long Island, Battle of, New York, N.Y., 1776—Juvenile literature. [1. Long Island, Battle of, New York, N.Y., 1776. 2. United States—History—Revolution, 1775-1783—Campaigns.] I. Title. II. Series.

E241.L8I54 2004
973.3'32—dc21   2002155065

Printed in China
10 9 8 7 6 5 4 3 2 1

CONTENTS

Preface: The American Revolution

Today, more than two centuries after the final shots were fired, the American Revolution remains an inspiring story not only to Americans, but also to people around the world. For many citizens, the well-known battles that occurred between 1775 and 1781—such as Lexington, Trenton, Yorktown, and others—represent the essence of the Revolution. In truth, however, the formation of the United States involved much more than the battles of the Revolutionary War. The creation of our nation occurred over several decades, beginning in 1763, at the end of the French and Indian War, and continuing until 1790, when the last of the original thirteen colonies ratified the Constitution.

More than two hundred years later, it may be difficult to fully appreciate the courage and determination of the people who fought for, and founded, our nation. The decision to declare independence was not made easily—and it was not unanimous. Breaking away from England—the ancestral land of most colonists—was a bold and difficult move. In addition to the emotional hardship of revolt, colonists faced the greatest military and economic power in the world at the time.

The first step on the path to the Revolution was essentially a dispute over money. By 1763 England's treasury had been drained in order to pay for the French and Indian War. British lawmakers, as well as England's new ruler, King George III, felt that the colonies should help to pay for the war's expense and for the cost of housing the British troops who remained in the colonies. Thus began a series of oppressive British tax acts and other laws that angered the colonists and eventually provoked full-scale violence.

The Stamp Act of 1765 was followed by the Townshend Acts in 1767. Gradually, colonists were forced to pay taxes on dozens of everyday goods from playing cards to paint to tea. At the same time, the colonists had no say in the passage of these acts. The more colonists complained that "taxation without representation is tyranny," the more British lawmakers claimed the right to make laws for the colonists "in all cases whatsoever." Soldiers and tax collectors were sent to the colonies to enforce the new laws. In addition, the colonists were forbidden to trade with any country but England.

Each act of Parliament pushed the colonies closer to unifying in opposition to English laws. Boycotts of British goods inspired protests and violence against tax collectors. Merchants who continued to trade with the Crown risked attacks by their colonial neighbors. The rising violence soon led to riots against British troops stationed in the colonies and the organized destruction of British goods. Tossing tea into Boston Harbor was just one destructive act. That event, the Boston Tea Party, led England to pass the so-called Intolerable Acts of 1774. The port of Boston was closed, more British troops were sent to the colonies, and many more legal rights for colonists were suspended.

Finally, there was no turning back. Early on an April morning in 1775, at Lexington Green in Massachusetts, the first shots of the American Revolution were fired. Even after the first battle, the idea of a war against England seemed unimaginable to all but a few radicals. Many colonists held out hope that a compromise could be reached. Except for the Battle of Bunker Hill and some minor battles at sea, the war ceased for much of 1775. During this time, delegates to the Continental Congress struggled to reach a consensus about the next step.

During those uncertain months, the Revolution was fought, not on a military battlefield, but on the battlefield of public opinion. Ardent rebels—especially Samuel Adams and Thomas Paine—worked tirelessly to keep the spirit of revolution alive. They stoked the fires of revolt by writing letters and pamphlets, speaking at public gatherings, organizing boycotts, and devising other forms of protest. It was their brave efforts that kept others focused on liberty and freedom until July 4, 1776. On that day, Thomas Jefferson's Declaration of Independence left no doubt about the intentions of the colonies. As John Adams wrote afterward, the "revolution began in hearts and minds not on battlefield."

As unifying as Jefferson's words were, the United States did not become a nation the moment the Declaration of Independence claimed the right of all people to "life, liberty, and the pursuit of happiness." Before, during, and after the war, Americans who spoke of their "country" still generally meant whatever colony was their home. Some colonies even had their own navies during the war, and a few sent their own representatives to Europe to seek aid for their colony alone while delegates from the Continental Congress were doing the same job for the whole United States. Real national unity did not begin to take hold until the inauguration of George Washington in 1789, and did not fully bloom until the dawn of the nineteenth century.

The Minuteman statue stands in Concord, Massachusetts.

The story of the American Revolution has been told for more than two centuries and may well be told for centuries to come. It is a tribute to the men and women who came together during this unique era that, to this day, people the world over find inspiration in the story of the Revolution. In the words of the Declaration of Independence, these great Americans risked "their lives, their fortunes, and their sacred honor" for freedom.

Introduction:
"A Most Vigorous Push"

On the sweltering afternoon of July 9, 1776, Patriot troops assembled on New York Island, today known as Manhattan, at the order of their commander, General George Washington. A week earlier, the Continental Congress in Philadelphia had approved the Declaration of Independence, and Washington wanted to read the document publicly to his troops. After more than a year of hostilities between patriot forces and the British army, the delegates in Philadelphia had made the official announcement: America considered itself independent from the rule of the British Crown.

Washington hoped that the declaration would boost the morale of his men, who had been in New York City since early spring. He believed that the declaration would help them to understand that they were Americans rather than individuals from separate colonies. As young men from Connecticut, Massachusetts, New Hampshire, and New York listened closely, Washington began with words that had been written by a thirty-three-year-old Virginian, Thomas Jefferson: "When in the course of human events, it becomes necessary for one people to dissolve the political bands that have connected them with another...."

Washington continued to read, and stated the rights common to all people, which included the right to "life, liberty, and the pursuit of happiness." Finally, Washington concluded with the vow made by the men who had signed the document: "We mutually pledge to each other our Lives, our Fortunes, and our sacred Honor."

6

The troops reacted with a joyous cheer. Several soldiers threw a rope around a huge statue of King George III in a city square and pulled it over. Men jeered the fallen likeness of the British king and boasted about driving the redcoats back across the Atlantic.

Washington could see that the declaration had inspired his men. Privately, however, he knew that it would take more than a piece of paper and high morale to defeat the greatest army in the world. That day, once again, he sent a request to Philadelphia for more gunpowder and reinforcements. Not only was his force low on ammunition, they were falling by the dozens to yellow fever.

In July 1776, General George Washington read the Declaration of Independence to patriot troops gathered on New York Island.

To add to his concerns, more than ten thousand British troops had landed in the previous week on Staten Island off the tip of Manhattan. He had no way of knowing it, but British ships with more than twenty thousand additional troops were headed for Staten Island from the southern colonies. Those additional troops would give the British army a force off New York that was larger than the population of the city itself.

Washington could sense that the British were determined to crush the new patriot army with overwhelming force as quickly as possible. He concluded his request with an emphasis on that point: "From every appearance they mean to make a most vigorous push to subdue [the colonies]."

Meeting at the Middle Colonies

S hortly after the Battle of Bunker Hill in June 1775, newly appointed General George Washington arrived in Massachusetts to take command of the army of what he called the "United Provinces of North America." Despite the fact that colonial troops had been forced to retreat in that battle, the British forces had suffered extremely heavy losses and had returned to their base in Boston. While on the way to his new command, Washington had received news of the battle. "The country is safe," Washington had said when he heard of the patriots' resistance. In truth, as bravely the patriots had fought, they were short of supplies and much of the army was made up of untrained recruits whose term of enlistment was set at three months.

The redcoats were too weakened by their losses, however, to attack the patriot base in Cambridge, west of Boston. Instead, the British troops, under command of General William Howe, fortified their position. Throughout the spring, the redcoats took in from the surrounding area more than one thousand colonists who supported the king. These people were called "Loyalists" or "Tories."

Washington arrived in early July and set up headquarters in Cambridge. His orders were to drill the various civilian volunteer units—called militia—and join them with his regulars into a unified fighting force. As groups were trained, he stationed them in a semicircle in the hills that ringed the Boston peninsula.

8

Although the redcoats were militarily strong enough to prevent direct invasion, they were in an extremely vulnerable position. Their only route of escape was by sea.

During his first weeks in command, Washington received word of a patriot victory at Fort Ticonderoga in northern New York near the Canadian border. More than fifty large British cannons had been captured, and Washington realized how valuable the big guns could be to his position. He assigned his twenty-five-year-old artillery commander, Colonel Henry Knox, to take a force and teams of oxen to New York and bring back the cannons.

Colonel Henry Knox transported British cannons captured in northern New York to Washington's army in Boston.

Throughout the final months of 1775, while volunteers streamed into Cambridge to enlist, Knox's force moved slowly northwest. The group reached Fort Ticonderoga in December, and the patriots built sleds on which to carry the cannons back to Boston. In late December, a force of two hundred men and four hundred oxen set off with fifty-nine cannons, each weighing almost a ton, on the three-hundred-mile return journey to Cambridge.

As the new year arrived, the British and Americans were at a stalemate. The British force was too weak to break out of its fortifications, and the patriot force was too weak to break into those same defenses. In February, Washington, frustrated by the standoff, proposed a direct attack across the ice of frozen Boston Harbor. The Massachusetts Committee of Safety, the patriot legislative body in that colony, refused to order the attack because they felt it was too dangerous. Washington, from a southern colony, had not yet earned the trust of many northern colonists.

9

Overwhelmed by Washington's forces, redcoats and Loyalists withdrew out of Boston Harbor.

In early March, after three months of travel over frozen rivers, along mud- and snow-covered trails, Knox and the big guns arrived. On March 5, the British troops and their Loyalist supporters saw that they were surrounded by a force of nearly twenty thousand patriots and almost sixty cannons. For Howe, the next step was obvious. He would have to begin an immediate withdrawal by sea. Redcoats and Loyalists filled transport ships. By March 27, the last of more than one hundred British ships under the command of Howe's brother, Admiral Richard Howe, sailed out of Boston Harbor. The ships set a course north for the Canadian province of Nova Scotia, a military stronghold in the British colonies.

In Boston, colonists celebrated the liberation of the city and the region. They had been under strict British control since the British had closed the port in 1774 to punish the colonists for destroying three shiploads of tea in an act of rebellion that became known as the Boston Tea Party. Washington, however, did not join in the celebration. Shortly before the British left, he had received word from a spy that Howe would remain in Nova Scotia only as long as it took to take on supplies and increase his troop strength. The British, Washington learned, had given up any hope of controlling Boston or the New England colonies. Their attention was now focused on the middle colonies, which were economically more valuable because of their farmlands and their warm-water ports.

10

Washington knew that this strategy almost certainly meant that Howe's army would attempt to take New York City. The city's location at the mouth of the Hudson River made it a key area. Control of the Hudson meant that British forces could come south from Canada to link up with Howe, a move that would cut off New England from sending forces south to any battles. New York City was also about one hundred miles from Philadelphia, the meeting place of the Continental Congress. Thus the British could use New York as a supply base for their army as they attacked Philadelphia. Finally, Washington knew, there was strong Loyalist support in and around New York. Unlike Boston, whose people generally hated British control, New York City could be a more friendly location for Howe's army.

By April 4, the entire patriot army was on the march to New York. Washington had a great deal of captured British artillery as well as roughly twenty thousand men in his army. More than half of them were in various state militias and were therefore more loyal to their colony or local commanders than to any central command. Almost all the men in the militia and the regular army were poorly trained, poorly equipped, and lacked discipline.

British general William Howe planned to take New York City to gain control of the Hudson River (pictured).

Many suffered from diseases such as yellow fever and were too ill to fight. The Americans marched south from Boston through Rhode Island to the seaport of New London, Connecticut. There, they boarded transport ships and sailed west down Long Island Sound to New York City.

Battle Lines are Drawn

Washington himself and his staff made the journey from Boston to New York by land and arrived in Manhattan, then known as New York Island, on April 14. Almost immediately, the general was faced with the same problem the leaders of the Continental Congress faced. Because the colonies had not officially declared independence, colonists in many areas continued to do business with the country Washington called the "enemy." Dozens of British vessels were anchored in New York Harbor, and local merchants supplied the ships as though nothing had occurred between the colonists and Britain over the previous year.

New York merchants supplied British ships docked in New York Harbor.

The Battle of Long Island

As his troops landed in New York, Washington angrily wrote to the New York Committee of Safety, the colony's ruling body. He pointed out the "glaring absurdity" of the merchants' actions, while his own poorly supplied troops built fortifications to protect the city from Howe's invasion. "In the cause of American liberty," he demanded that the committee take steps to stop the "evil" and ban all relations between New York merchants and the British ships.

Washington's stern letter forced the committee to agree to his demand. Throughout the spring of 1776, patriot forces continued to fortify New York City. On the southern part of the island, in an area that became known as the Battery, they constructed earthworks for the artillery that Knox had captured. In addition, a heavily fortified enclosure named Fort Washington was built on the island's northern tip.

★

In 1776, the American ship *Alfred*, under Captain John Paul Jones, captured eight British merchant ships.

★

The Hudson River formed a natural barrier that protected the patriots on the western side of New York Island. On the eastern side, Washington decided to station his troops across the East River in an area known as the Brooklyn Heights. This area was located at the far western tip of Long Island. Washington placed his largest and most well-trained force at Brooklyn Heights. About four thousand troops, under the command of General Nathanael Greene, were placed on high ground from which they could overlook Brooklyn and New York Island.

Meanwhile, British forces were also active. By mid-June, a fleet under Admiral Richard Howe sailed south from Nova Scotia, just as Washington had expected. On June 29, the fleet sailed into the waters off of New York. It was the largest single force Britain had ever sent into action. More than ten thousand soldiers on nearly one hundred transport ships were accompanied by thirty warships with a total of twelve hundred guns. Americans on shore were awestruck by the sight of the force. Daniel McCurtin, a young patriot soldier from Maryland,

13

New York City in 1776

★ ★ ★ ★ ★

Today, New York City has five boroughs separated by waterways. Brooklyn and Queens are located on the western end of Long Island, which is separated from the island of Manhattan by the East River. Staten Island and Manhattan are separate landmasses. Finally, Bronx, to the north, is part of the New York State mainland. In colonial times, however, New York City was little more than a small town surrounded by farms called "bowers."

To early Dutch explorers, Manhattan Island—named for its Native American inhabitants—was an ideal place for settlement. The nine-mile-long island, located at the meeting point of several large waterways, became the Dutch settlement of New Amsterdam in 1624. In the 1660s, England

Colonial New York's harborside (pictured) bustled with trade between local merchants and the British.

took control of the island and surrounding region, and the land was named after the Duke of York, brother to King Charles II. Manhattan became New York Island, and it was this twenty-seven-square-mile piece of land people knew as New York City.

Although many New York colonists opposed British policies such as the Stamp Act, the city did not have the same anti-British feeling as Boston. Many settlers in New York had strong ties to the British crown. A large number owned farms and had become wealthy in trade with England. In addition, because New York's harbor did not freeze in winter, as Boston's did, the city was better for merchants to trade in goods and products. As a result, the move for independence from England was not as widely supported in New York as it was in other colonies.

By the summer of 1776, New York City had largely been abandoned by civilian residents. Patriot soldiers, who had taken over the island, had chopped down fences and orchards to make gun emplacements and barricades. The royal governor of New York had fled to a British ship in New York Harbor. Most Loyalists had left the city and gone to outlying areas, including Long Island.

described the arrival of the British fleet in his diary: "I could not believe my eyes.... In about 10 minutes the whole bay was full of shipping as ever it could be.... I thought all London was afloat."

A week after the British arrival in New York, the Continental Congress in Philadelphia approved the Declaration of Independence. Copies of the document were printed and distributed throughout the colonies. While the British forces constructed a base off the southern tip of Manhattan on Staten Island, Washington read the declaration to his troops on July 9. As his men celebrated, Washington wrote to the congress about the weak state of his army due to illness and the lack of supplies. He mentioned the enormous force on Staten Island. He did not know that over the following month, the huge force would actually triple in size.

Throughout June, at the same time the British were in New York, an even larger British army had arrived in the port of Charleston, South Carolina, having sailed directly from England. That force, under generals Henry Clinton and Charles Cornwallis, was assigned to take control of the port, the largest in the southern colonies.

The Continental Congress signed the Declaration of Independence just one week after British troops arrived in New York.

15

The British forces at Charleston, however, were beaten by patriot forces in a battle on Sullivan's Island in the center of the harbor. Clinton, who had also been a leader of the British forces at Bunker Hill, decided to abandon Charleston and sail north to join Howe. Over a period of six weeks in July and early August, more than twenty thousand additional troops under Clinton and Cornwallis joined the large force camped on Staten Island, which brought the total to about thirty-two thousand. Among the soldiers were eight thousand troops from Germany, called Hessians, who were hired by the king to fight for the British. The Hessians were fierce fighters who, unlike most other soldiers of the day, did not believe in taking prisoners. By mid-August, more than five hundred ships sat at anchor on New York Harbor.

Admiral Richard Howe (above) and his brother, General William Howe (below), coordinated their forces in the early days of the battle.

Despite the size of his force, Howe decided against a direct attack on the patriots in New York City. He had commanded British forces at Bunker Hill and had lost hundreds of his soldiers in such an attack, so he was reluctant to attempt the same strategy again. Instead, Howe decided to sail south from Staten Island across the Verrazano Narrows, the place where the Hudson and East Rivers meet the Atlantic Ocean. Howe's destination was Long Island. The 118-mile long, 20-mile wide region was a Loyalist stronghold and an area of huge potato fields and large livestock farms. Howe knew that control of Long Island would allow him to keep his massive army supplied with food for as long as it took to defeat the patriots.

On Thursday, August 22, 1776, Howe assembled a force of more than twenty thousand troops, including five thousand Hessian soldiers. Over a period of six hours, Admiral Howe's ships transported his brother's troops from Staten Island across Gravesend Bay on the south shore of Long Island. The battle plan called for them to march

The Plot to Assassinate Washington

Washington's demand that Loyalists cease all interaction with British ships infuriated many New York colonists. Almost as soon as Washington had sent a letter that contained the demand to the New York Committee on Safety, a plot was devised to kill him and his senior staff officers. Almost one hundred men, mainly from Long Island, were involved in the plot. One of those most closely tied to the plan was one of Washington's personal guards, an eighteen-year-old named Thomas Hickey.

The plan was set to be put into action in late June at the same time as Howe's force arrived from Nova Scotia. A report issued at the time explained, "Upon the arrival of the British troops, they [the American Loyalists] were to murder [Washington and] all the staff officers, blow up the [ammunition] magazines, and secure the town."

As it happened, Hickey was arrested in May for the possession of counterfeit money. While in jail, Hickey bragged about the plan to his cellmate, another counterfeiter. The cellmate quickly exchanged the information in return for his freedom.

By the time the British sailed into New York Harbor in late June, the plot had been uncovered. On June 28, a crowd of twenty thousand soldiers gathered to watch Hickey hang for his part in it. After the execution, patriot militiamen from Long Island were sent across the region to arrest a list of Loyalist sympathizers who had hidden in the woods, brush, and swamps there. Most had, by then, fled the area, and only six of the plotters were arrested. All were imprisoned, but none were executed.

A story that was well known in those days but never verified told of Washington being sent a plate of poisoned peas at his headquarters. His housekeeper suspected that something was wrong with the peas and threw them to the chickens in the yard. All of the chickens who ate the peas immediately died.

Washington himself never wrote of the poisoned peas. After Hickey's execution, however, he wrote to Congress, "I am hopeful this example will produce many salutary [positive] consequences, and deter others from entering into the like traitorous practices."

north and attack Greene's force of four thousand men at Brooklyn Heights. At about that same time, Washington had divided his force on New York Island and accompanied about two thousand additional men across the East River to reinforce Greene.

The Battle of Long Island

The main patriot defensive position at Brooklyn Heights was a series of forts and trenches, called redoubts, which ran from Wallabout Bay on the north to Gowanus Bay on the south, a distance of slightly more than a mile. Several miles southeast of Brooklyn Heights stood a ridge of thickly forested hills—some nearly two hundred feet high—called the Heights of Guan.

Several days before Howe's move, Greene had fallen ill from the yellow fever that swept through the patriot forces. Washington replaced Greene with General Israel Putnam of Connecticut. Putnam, a lifelong military man, had distinguished himself at the Battle of Bunker Hill. Unfortunately for Washington and the patriot forces, though, Putnam had no knowledge of the local terrain, and the few maps available were unreliable.

Putnam followed Washington's orders to set up outer defenses at three passes along the Heights of Guan. Neither Putnam nor the other patriot leaders, however, knew that the Heights actually had four passes that connected the western island with the eastern end. Putnam failed to put any defenders at the fourth pass, Jamaica Pass, on his left flank.

Howe, on the other hand, knew about Jamaica Pass thanks to Loyalist spies in the area. When these spies told Howe that the patriots had left Jamaica Pass unguarded, he ordered most of the British force to march north toward it. To create a diversion, Howe also ordered attacks by two smaller forces against the guarded passes. These smaller attacks, Howe believed, would fool the patriots about the main attack. The largest British force would then circle behind the patriots and surround them.

In the summer of 1776, demand for Thomas Paine's pamphlet *Common Sense* grew faster than copies could be printed.

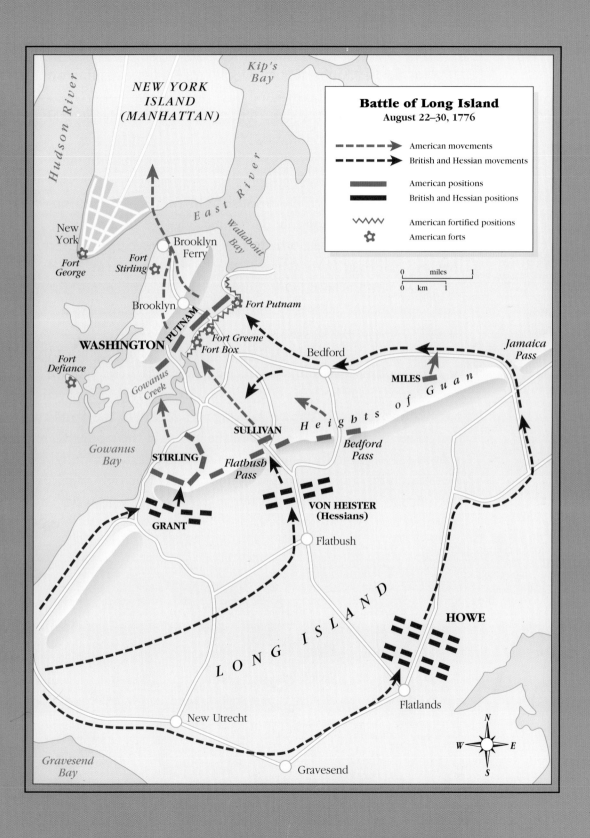

Battle of Long Island
August 22–30, 1776

American movements
British and Hessian movements
American positions
British and Hessian positions
American fortified positions
American forts

0 miles 1
0 km 1

Kip's Bay

NEW YORK ISLAND (MANHATTAN)

Hudson River

East River

Wallabout Bay

New York

Fort George

Fort Stirling

Brooklyn Ferry

Brooklyn

PUTNAM

WASHINGTON

Fort Defiance

Gowanus Creek

Fort Putnam

Fort Greene
Fort Box

Bedford

Heights of Guan

Jamaica Pass

MILES

SULLIVAN

Flatbush Pass

Bedford Pass

STIRLING

Gowanus Bay

GRANT

VON HEISTER
(Hessians)

Flatbush

HOWE

New Utrecht

Flatlands

L O N G   I S L A N D

Gravesend Bay

Gravesend

N
W   E
S

At his field headquarters in Brooklyn Heights, Washington did not know of the unguarded pass or of Howe's plan. He did know, however, that his army would soon face battle for the first time under his command. He worried about how his inexperienced troops would react against an overwhelming force. In an attempt to encourage his men, he wrote a message that his officers read to the troops: "The time is now near at hand, which must probably determine whether Americans are to be freemen or slaves; whether they are to have any property they can call their own; whether their homes and farms are to be . . . destroyed. The fate of . . . millions will now depend, under God, on the conduct and courage of this army. . . . We have therefore to resolve to conquer or die."

Late on the night of August 26, Howe personally took charge of a force of ten thousand troops, with support from Clinton and Cornwallis. The British, guided by local Loyalists, moved north along the road known as King's Highway to the Jamaica Pass. The full moon was bright in the sky, and the troops were able to march quickly along the rutted roads in the moonlight. The march through the pass was uneventful. The only patriots the redcoats encountered were five men on patrol who were captured without a single shot fired.

Major Mordecai Gist's rear guard provided cover fire so that fellow patriots could safely retreat.

At dawn on August 27, cannons signaled the British to begin the frontal attack on the patriots. Hessians under General Philip von Heister attacked the center of the patriots defense at Flatbush Pass. At the same time, about five thousand troops under General James Grant attacked the right flank at Narrows Road at a location marked by a tavern called the Red Lion Inn. Shortly after those attacks were launched, Howe's ten thousand soldiers suddenly appeared from Jamaica Pass and overwhelmed the lightly defended left flank.

Howe's plan caught the patriots by complete surprise. The patriots were nearly surrounded by 9:00 A.M. "[W]e were ordered to attempt a retreat by fighting our way through the enemy, who had . . . nearly filled every field and road between us and our lines [at Brooklyn Heights]," wrote an American soldier. "We had not retreated a quarter of a mile before we were fired upon by an advanced part of the enemy, and those upon our rear were playing upon us with their artillery."

The Hessian attack at the center was fierce. The well-trained Germans killed any Americans who tried to surrender. "The greater part of their riflemen were pierced to the trees with bayonets," wrote a Hessian officer.

By 11:00 A.M. the rout was almost complete. Patriots dropped their weapons and fled from the slaughter. Michael Graham, an eighteen-year-old private, wrote, "It is impossible for me to describe the confusion and horror of the scene . . . our men running in almost every direction, and run which way they would, they were almost sure to meet the British or Hessians. And the enemy huzzahing when they took prisoners made it truly a day of distress to the Americans."

The disaster would have been worse if not for the courage of a regiment of four hundred to five hundred men from Maryland. These men, commanded by Major Mordecai Gist, were among the few who made an orderly retreat that day from

★

In August 1776, John Paul Jones was commissioned in Philadelphia as the captain of the American warship *Providence*.

★

21

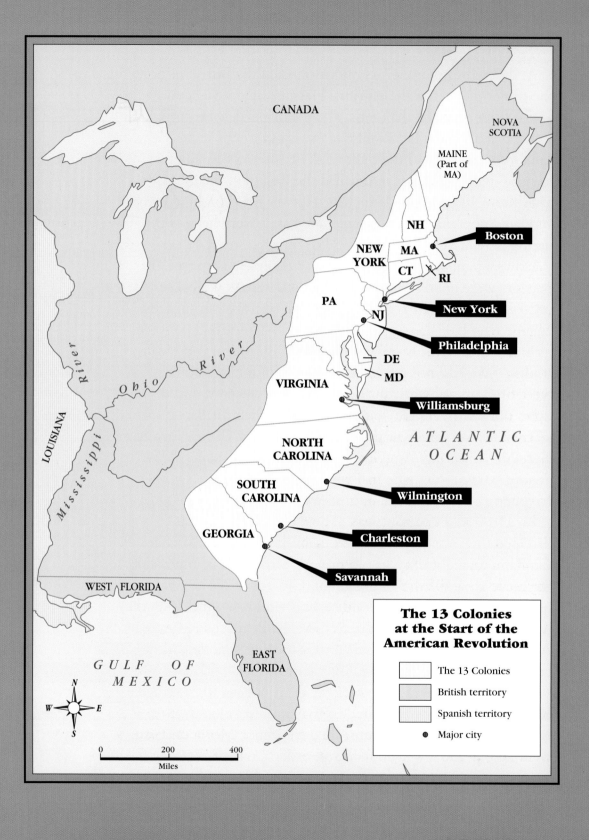

CANADA

NOVA
SCOTIA

MAINE
(Part of
MA)

NH

NEW
YORK

MA

Boston

CT

RI

PA

NJ

New York

Philadelphia

DE

MD

VIRGINIA

Williamsburg

NORTH
CAROLINA

*ATLANTIC
OCEAN*

SOUTH
CAROLINA

Wilmington

GEORGIA

Charleston

Savannah

WEST FLORIDA

EAST
FLORIDA

*G U L F   O F
M E X I C O*

Mississippi River

Ohio   River

LOUISIANA

N
W   E
S

0   200   400

Miles

The 13 Colonies
at the Start of the
American Revolution

	The 13 Colonies
	British territory
	Spanish territory
●	Major city

Almost one thousand patriots died in the British attack on Brooklyn Heights.

the right flank. While bullets and cannonballs whistled around them, they formed a rear guard and held off the advance of British troops while their comrades escaped. As the British circle closed behind them, Cornwallis and a large detachment of redcoats took control of a stone farmhouse, the Cortelyou house. The structure was built beside Mill Dam Road and a bridge that provided the only escape route from the right flank back to the patriot encampment at Brooklyn Heights.

In order to keep Cornwallis's men from picking off the patriots as they ran past, patriot general William Alexander, also known as Lord Stirling, ordered Gist and his men to attack the Cortelyou House. The attack, Alexander hoped, would occupy the British long enough for the other patriots to retreat across the Mill Dam Bridge. For almost three hours, from 11:00 A.M. until nearly 2:00 P.M., the Marylanders counterattacked until superior British numbers forced them to scatter. More than 250 men of the regiment were killed or wounded in the fight.

Many in the heroic unit were forced to swim for their lives across Mill Dam Pond to safety. Only a few Maryland troops who could swim and who were lucky enough to avoid being shot in the water made it back. A seventeen-year-old Connecticut soldier, Joseph Plumb Martin, later wrote of the Maryland men: "When they came out of the water and mud to us, looking like water rats, it was a truly pitiful sight. Many of them were killed in the pond and many were drowned."

23

The patriots fled the Long Island battlefields after their defeat by the British.

Washington, meanwhile, had ordered reinforcements from New York Island, but they arrived too late to participate in the battle. Despite the fact that the patriot force still numbered about 9,000 with the reinforcements, they were trapped by the redcoat army and by British warships waiting at the mouth of the East River. By 2:00 P.M., the battle was over. By that time, British forces had lost about 400 men—63 men and 337 wounded. The patriots had about 970 men killed or wounded and about 1,100 taken prisoner.

Although the patriots were badly weakened and could have been easily overwhelmed, Howe refused the requests of his staff to continue the attack. Once again, Howe hesitated, recalling the heavy losses at Bunker Hill. He also believed that with his brother's fleet at the mouth of the East River, it would be a simple matter to destroy the patriots once favorable winds allowed the ships to sail up the river. In his refusal to press the attack, Howe told his officers that the patriot army "could be had at a cheap price."

Fortunately for Washington and the defeated patriots, however, strong winds blew down the East River that day and prevented Admiral Howe from sailing his large ships up the river. As dusk approached, Washington knew that if the wind

24

changed, the patriots' dreams of independence would be shattered by British cannons and bayonets.

The Miraculous Escape

The strong winds that prevented Howe from sailing up the East River continued throughout the day on August 27. The next day, those same winds blew in a fierce storm. The trenches of both the British and American soldiers became muddy holes. Clothes were soaked and gunpowder was too wet to ignite. Men had to sleep without tents.

In his headquarters on Brooklyn Heights, Washington wrestled with a plan to rescue his army from certain disaster. On the afternoon of August 28, he met with his top officers. The division of the patriot force between Brooklyn and Manhattan, Washington said, left both points at risk. The only chance was to evacuate to New York City across the East River.

The evacuation of almost half of the patriot army from under the watchful eyes of the British, however, would be difficult. Colonel Benjamin Tallmadge, one of Washington's senior officers, later wrote that "to move so large a body of troops with all their necessary appendages [equipment] across a river a full mile wide, with a rapid current, in the face of a victorious, well-disciplined army nearly three times as numerous seemed . . . to present most formidable obstacles."

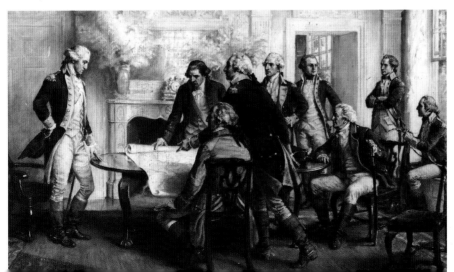

Washington and his advisers decided to evacuate their Brooklyn troops across the East River to join patriot forces in New York City.

Part of the plan involved deception. As darkness fell, Washington had about fifteen hundred men at front of the patriot fortifications create noises that suggested they were about to assault the British lines six hundred yards away. Meanwhile, Washington's other troops quietly left their positions and marched to the river. Martin wrote in his journal:

> We were strictly [forbidden] to speak, or even cough, while on the march. All orders were given from officer to officer, and communicated to the men in whispers. What such secrecy could mean we could not divine [figure out].

The task of ferrying the army across the strong currents of the East River was assigned to a man for whom Washington had the greatest respect—Colonel John Glover of Massachusetts. Glover commanded a rugged, well-trained unit of seamen from Marblehead, a fishing community north of Boston. The so-called "Men of Marblehead" were among the most admired of all fighting units in the Revolution. A patriot officer who was highly critical of the military attitude of most recruits wrote, "[T]he only exception I recollect to have seen to the miserably constituted bands [recruits] was the regiment of Glover. There was an appearance of discipline in this corps."

In just one night, Colonel John Glover and his disciplined seamen ferried almost ten thousand patriot soldiers across the East River.

Washington believed that Glover was the only man who could get the patriot army out of the critical situation it faced. Glover's unit had a number of flat-bottom transport boats, but not enough to move a large force. To assist in the evacuation, Washington ordered his supply officer "to impress [take over] every kind of craft on either side of New York" that had oars or sails.

With a few additional boats for the task, Glover's men began a night of backbreaking work, all to be accomplished in complete silence. They began about ten o'clock. The full moon that had helped Howe two nights earlier was covered by thick clouds that prevented the British on land from observing any movement. The darkness also kept the movement of the boats hidden from lookouts on the British ships. Regiment after regiment of wet and weary patriots left the trenches and marched to the boats. Washington knew that the summer night would not remain dark for long. Any troops left on Long Island at dawn would be captured. Nevertheless, he believed in Glover, whom he called a "tough little terrier of a man."

At first, the winds allowed the boats to use sails, and they swiftly made round trips between Brooklyn and New York Island. When the winds died down, Glover's men rowed with the boats' oarlocks muffled in canvas to keep them silent. The boats were so heavily loaded that there were only a few inches between the water and the upper edges of the craft. Yet the water was smooth enough to prevent any mishaps.

Washington ordered every kind of boat available to be used in the evacuation.

The weather also seemed to be on the patriots' side for the risky mission. In the early morning hours of August 30, the

John Glover

The man Washington described as a "tough little terrier" remains one of the forgotten heroes of the Revolution. John Glover was born in 1732 in Salem, Massachusetts. At 21, Glover moved to the fishing community of Marblehead. There he opened a shop and began to save his money until he had enough to buy a small ship. As the captain of a merchant vessel, he earned enough to purchase more ships.

John Glover

In the years that led to the Revolution, Glover was active in the patriot cause. He formed a militia unit to oppose any British invasion. In addition to his militia unit, Glover offered his ships to the war. The Hannah, the first ship to sail in the service of the new United States, was Glover's own schooner. During the long siege of Boston, the Hannah sailed the waters around Boston Harbor and harassed British transport ships. Glover was so successful that Washington asked Glover to outfit two more ships and form what came to be known as "Washington's Navy."

When the need for a well-trained crew of seaman arose after the defeat at Long Island, Washington immediately called on Glover. That heroic effort was just the first of several events in late 1776 that made Glover one of Washington's most valuable officers. The event that made him most famous, however, occurred in December.

One well-known image of the war is that of Washington crossing the icy Delaware River on December 30, 1776. Washington and his force crossed the river to surprise the Hessian troops camped at Trenton, New Jersey. Glover and his men were at the oars and the poles of the boats that carried Washington across the river. Once on land, the Men of Marblehead fought to defeat the Hessians. They then carried nine hundred captured prisoners back across the Delaware to the patriot prison camp. After the victory, Washington promoted Glover to general for his part in the battle. Glover died in 1798, a year before Washington.

fierce two-day storm ended, but heavy clouds remained to hide the activity. When the wind blew away the cloud cover, a heavy fog settled on the Long Island shore, but left the New York shore clear. Thus the troops were hidden as they left, but Glover's sailors could clearly see the landing on the opposite shore.

There were more Loyalists than patriots in New York during the war.

The escape under the noses of the British was one of Washington's most brilliant moves. It was an action that tremendously increased the respect in which his troops held him. Throughout the night, as troops assembled at the Brooklyn shore, they saw Washington on his horse. The general, exhausted after three sleepless nights, refused to leave until every last man was safely across the water.

"There never was a man that behaved better upon the occasion than General Washington," a soldier wrote in a letter to a New York newspaper. "He was on horseback the whole night, and never left the ferry stairs till he had seen the whole of his troops embarked."

As dawn broke on August 30, a British unit on patrol realized that the patriot front lines were unguarded. British soldiers quickly charged the patriot trenches only to find them deserted. The redcoats continued to the shore of the East River just as the sun burned through the fog. They arrived in time to see the last of Glover's boats leave. Shots were fired and four Americans were wounded. Those were the only casualties suffered throughout the evacuation.

Washington's trust in the abilities of Glover and the Men of Marblehead was well placed. In a little more than nine hours they had carried almost ten thousand men, along with supplies, cannon, and animals, out from under British guns. The action saved the patriot army and the Revolution. Some military historians feel that Washington's retreat was equal in its brilliance to Howe's total victory two days before.

Among the last patriot soldiers to leave the lines was Tallmadge. After the Revolution, he wrote:

29

In the history of warfare, I do not recollect a more fortunate retreat. After all, the providential appearance of the fog saved a part of our army from being captured, and certainly myself, among others who formed the rear guard. Gen. Washington has never received credit which was due to him for this wise and most fortunate measure.

By late morning on August 30, the wind had shifted. Howe sent ten British frigates and twenty gunboats up the river. Like the land-based troops of his brother, however, the ships arrived too late.

Epilogue

With the evacuation of Brooklyn Heights, Long Island fell under complete control of the British. It remained in British hands for the entire Revolution, and the flat, fertile farmland served as a food basket for the redcoats throughout the war. Howe's secretary, who kept a journal, wrote an entry on September 6 that stated:

The fleet & army are now exceedingly well supplied with fresh provisions & vegetables from Long Island, which is a pleasing circumstance both for the health & spirit of the troops. The Hessians, in particular, never fared so well before, and seem remarkably happy in their situation. Add to all this, the trees are so loaded with apples, that they seem to defy all the powers of a fair consumption.

For the patriot army, the good fortune of the escape soon ended. By mid-September 16, they were forced to abandon New York Island, and by late fall, they were in full retreat across New Jersey toward Philadelphia. Some of the darkest days of the American Revolution were about to begin for the patriots.

Glossary

artillery mounted guns, usually cannons, positioned on land
bayonet a long knife-like weapon attached to the end of a musket or rifle
flank the side of a fighting position
evacuation a mass movement of troops from a military position
fortification something constructed for defense
Loyalists American colonists who remained loyal to England
militia a civilian fighting force
patriots soldiers who fought against the British in the American Revolution
peninsula land surrounded on three sides by water
redcoats nickname given to British soldiers
strategy a plan of action

For More Information

Books

Ketchum, Richard. *Divided Loyalties: How the Revolution Came to New York*. New York, NY: Henry Holt, 2002.

Lefkowtitz, Arthur. *The Long Retreat*. Bloomington, IN: Upland Press, 1998.

Schecter, Barnett. *The Battle for New York*. New York, NY: Walker and Company, 1995.

Smith, Carter. *The Revolutionary War: A Sourcebook on Colonial America* (American Albums from the Collections of the Library of Congress). Brookfield, CT: Millbrook Press, 1991.

Websites

Long Island History
http://www.lihistory.com
One of the best websites available on the battle, with maps

The American Revolution
http://www.theamericanrevolution.org/battles/bat_bhil.asp
A website of the entire war with specific details about Long Island and other battles as well good biographies and primary source material

31

Index